THAT WAS CALLED
PASSION

THAT WAS
CALLED
PASSION

Inspiring Thoughts
of JOHN D. BECK

compiled by Elizabeth Lynch

16th Street Press

Proceeds from sales of this book are donated to
"Spotlights," the Patrons of Escanaba Schools
Performing Arts, in Escanaba, Michigan.
Donations are welcome and may be sent to
Spotlights
P.O. Box 965
Escanaba, MI 49829.

16th Street Press
322 S. 16th Street, Escanaba, MI 49829

To John D. Beck

Thank you

*for helping us
to learn as students,
sing as musicians,
and grow as people.*

Introduction

Teacher. Choir director. Striver after excellence. Master motivator.

All of these words describe John D. Beck, director of choral music of Escanaba Schools for almost 40 years. Chances are, if you're holding this book in your hands, you have sung under Mr. Beck's direction at some point in time or worked alongside him in music or education. If so, the words you'll read and the passion behind them should sound pretty familiar (and, I hope, bring back some nice memories). If you don't know John, you're in for a treat. For, without necessarily trying to be inspiring in a dramatic sort of way, the encouragements (and, yes, corrections) he offers throughout rehearsals really *are* very inspiring in a way that comes quite naturally to him.

For a bit of biographical info, for his nearly four decades as a music educator John has led thousands of young people to grow musically and as people. His choirs and smaller ensembles routinely achieve first division ratings at state-level festivals, and a number of his groups have been chosen to sing in the prestigious Michigan Youth Arts Festival. His commitment to musical achievement and personal growth led John's colleagues to choose him as director of the Michigan High School State Honors Choir in 2014. Quite an honor! But also no surprise to those of us who know him.

As for this book, growing up I took piano lessons from Kim Beck, John's wife; so to me Mr. Beck was just the bearded man who was always at the piano recitals. However, when I started chorus class in ninth grade, I began to realize how much more there was to him. Not only was he teaching us how to be musical, but he was also giving us advice on how to live with purpose, something I found to be worth sharing. So I started writing down some of his most inspiring words. For four years I have been collecting these quotes, discreetly jotting them down as I heard them, in hopes of someday making a gift for Mr. Beck. And here it is! At the end of senior year, with some assistance from 16th Street Press, we created this book and presented it to Mr. Beck as a thank-you present at the 2016 spring concert.

So, no, he didn't know I was doing this; but yes, he has been gracious enough to let the book be offered to the public. After expenses, all profits will be going to benefit Spotlights, the "booster club" of the performing arts at Escanaba High School. If you'd like to make an additional contribution, you'll find the address on the copyright page.

Enough introduction already. Let's get to John Beck's words about beauty and excellence and passion. I hope you find them as inspiring as I have.

Lizzy Lynch
May 2016

THAT WAS CALLED
PASSION

We are *real* people

giving *real* music

to other *real* people.

I don't want to be good.

I want to be amazing.

I want this to

hurt my ears with

beauty.

In all your classes you learn things for your brain.

In this class you learn feeling things and emotion things.

Make it be

musical moments

of beauty and joy.

If you *fake* it,

it might become *real*.

The details of

excellence are

difficult and dull.

Do I hate you?

No, I don't.

Do you need to do the right thing?

Yes, you do.

Am I going to teach it to you?

Yes, by whatever it takes.

The notes are just suggestions.

You have to add the

passion.

Don't accept not being

completely accurate.

And the *heavens* burst

open

and we sang.

Be **MAGICIANS** of

sound.

Don't ever be "kind of."

"Kind of" kind of sucks.

It's not about
what
you sing.

It's about
how
you sing it.

The more you hear music,

the more you become

the music you hear.

We know we took
people to another place

and sometimes that's
more important

than all the other
accolades and awards.

We don't have time
to be wimpy.

Listen

and make that

a part of you.

That's exactly what

singing is:

musical fireworks.

In life

we don't stand in

sections.

It was insanely *good*.

It can be insanely *better*.

You can't take a

SHORTCUT

to success.

You have to ask yourself what's important:

that we learn or that we get a good score?

I'm not being a jerk.

I'm just trying to be good.

Realize the difference.

As a teacher,

I'm trying to pull out

passion and *excitement*

about real things in life.

It doesn't make you
smart
to appear smart.

Paint the words with your voice.

Make your voice the
paintbrush.

People have to work hard

to sound effortless.

You're doing
really great.

That's why I'm pushing
you to the next level.

It's not wrong to try to be

AMAZING.

This is what I think is most important.

We don't want them to leave and think, "Oh, that was nice."

We want them to leave and feel different.

And we have the power to do that.

Great voices have been

brought to shame by

flatness.

ARTICULATION

is

ATTITUDE.

When we get the

groove,

everything just flows in

life.

Here you thought you
had a blow-off class.

More like a
blow-your-mind class.

Sing like you're

IMPORTANT.

Are we good?

Yeah.

But I always want to get one step further.

We're not doing this for the scores.

We're doing this because it's what makes us better.

Isn't it cool

to be

musical?

People always go,

"Oh, it'll come together."

No, it doesn't always just
come together.

It comes together
because we work.

I don't want to be
reigning you in.

I want to be *dancing*.

The notes are only so

much of the world

of beautiful, passionate

music.

It's weird.

We work and work and
work and work

and all of a sudden we
get to a place

where it starts to be
special.

You have to

practice

to rehearse.

It's not okay to just sing notes.

Ever.

That's why I do this:

for that one
freaking
moment

that makes you go
to a different place.

Working hard at details is boring

but it's necessary if you really want to be

something special.

The bottom line is

music is supposed to be
fun

and if you go up there
and don't have fun,

then you missed the
whole point.

Don't accept that we
kind of know it

because then it could
be that much better.

Do you see sound?

I do.

Not everyone

is smart enough

to get to that other
place

that music gets to

but that's what we're
doing.

We're great

but I'm trying to go
over the top

because we can go
over the top.

It's not starting to be good.

It's starting to be *special*.

Hey, shut up.

I'm complimenting you.

Life is not always written

in the *key of C*.

That was not called anger.

That was called passion.